W9-ALN-017

Rectangles

Teddy Borth

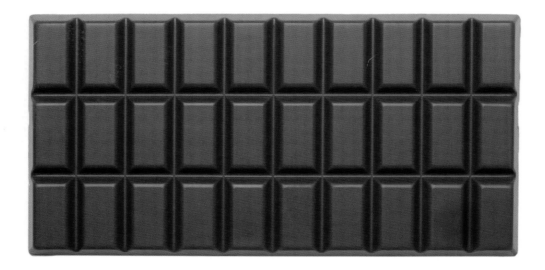

Abdo
SHAPES ARE FUN!
Kids

abdopublishing.com

Published by Abdo Kids, a division of ABDO, PO Box 398166, Minneapolis, Minnesota 55439.
Copyright © 2016 by Abdo Consulting Group, Inc. International copyrights reserved in all countries.
No part of this book may be reproduced in any form without written permission from the publisher.

Printed in the United States of America, North Mankato, Minnesota.

102015

012016

 THIS BOOK CONTAINS
RECYCLED MATERIALS

Photo Credits: Glow Images, iStock, Shutterstock

Production Contributors: Teddy Borth, Jennie Forsberg, Grace Hansen

Design Contributors: Candice Keimig, Dorothy Toth

Library of Congress Control Number: 2015941979

Cataloging-in-Publication Data

Borth, Teddy.

 Rectangles / Teddy Borth.

   p. cm. -- (Shapes are fun!)

ISBN 978-1-68080-145-3 (lib. bdg.)

Includes index.

1. Rectangles--Juvenile literature. 2. Geometry--Juvenile literature. 3. Shapes--Juvenile literature.   I. Title.

516/.15--dc23

2015941979

Table of Contents

Rectangles

A rectangle has 4 sides.

It has 4 angles.

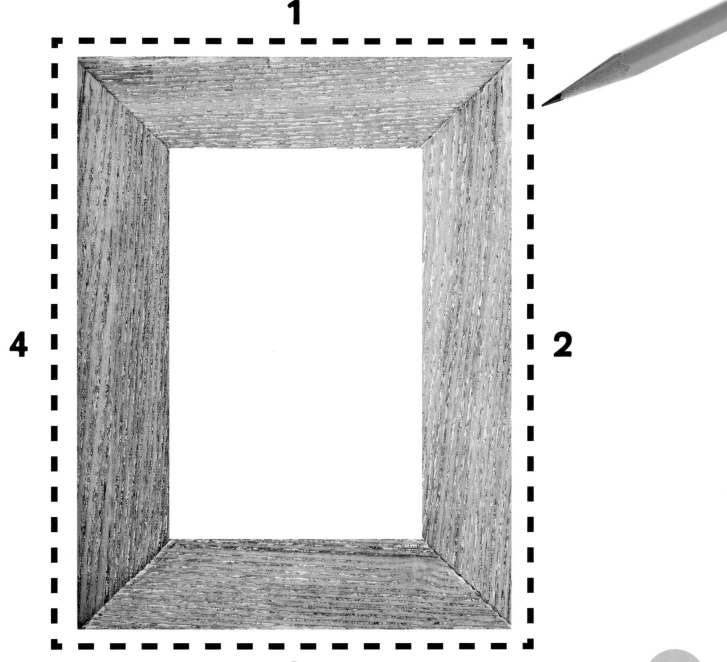

1

2

3

4

5

This shape is found all over!

They are on soccer fields.

They show where to play.

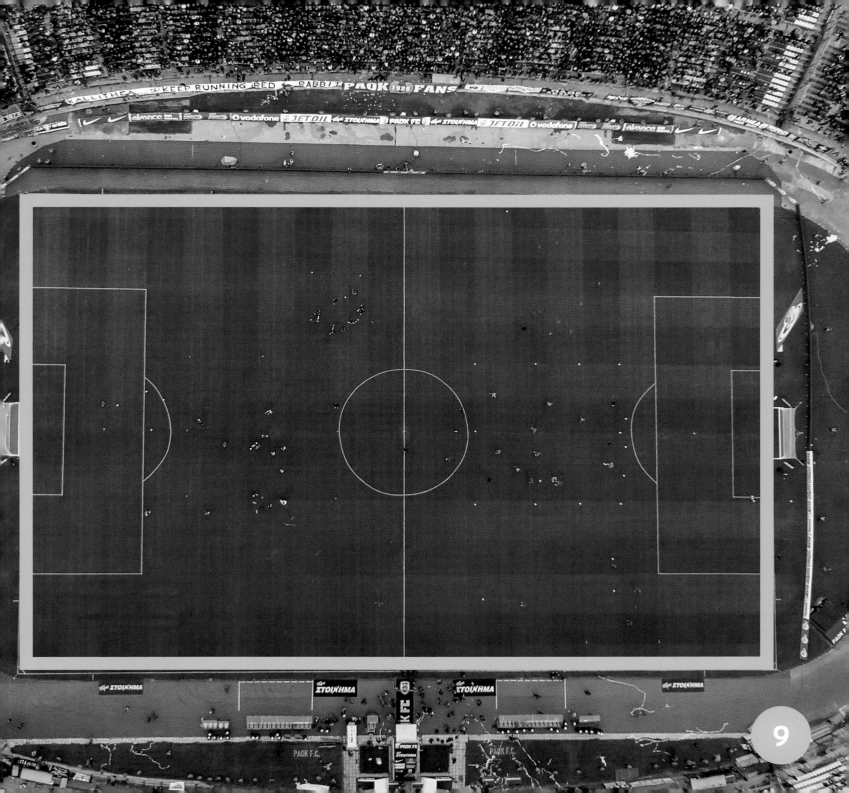

They are on screens.

Beth uses her tablet.

People swim in them.

They are on school buses.

They let James on.

They pile neatly.

They make a wall.

They are on books.

Sara holds one.

19

Look around you!

You will find a rectangle.

Count the Rectangles!

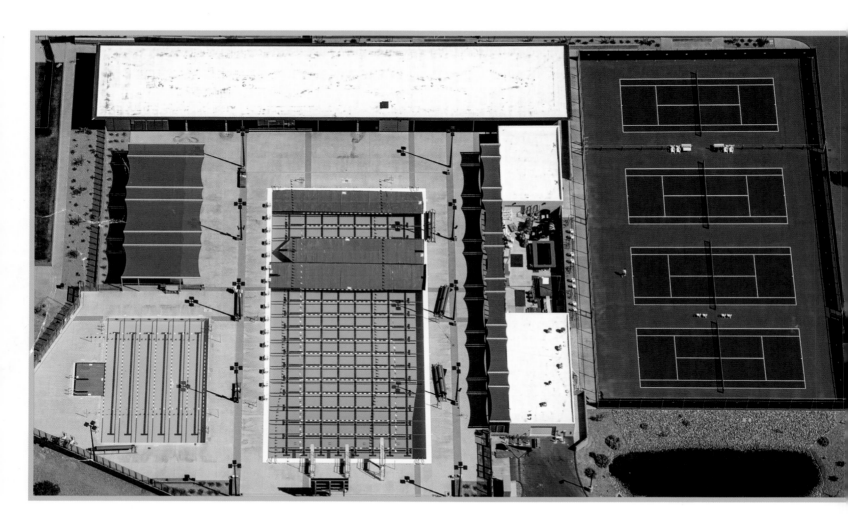

Glossary

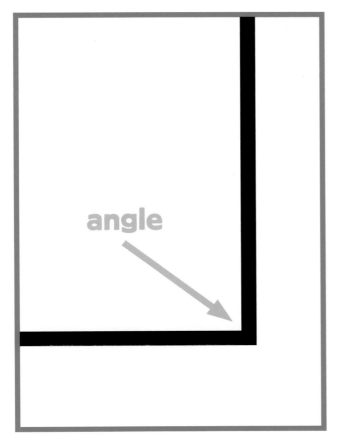

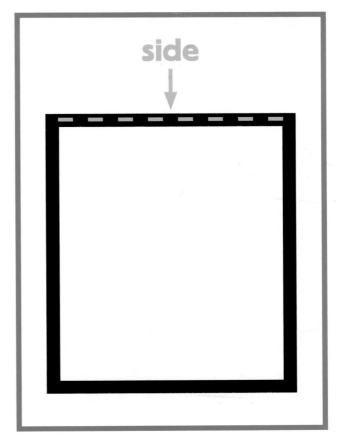

angle
the corner where two lines come together.

side
a line forming a border of an object.

Index

abdokids.com

Use this code to log on to abdokids.com and access crafts, games, videos, and more!

Abdo Kids Code:
SRK1453